U N W

- 2 0 2 1 -

A Co-creation from Marlena K. McGuigan

+

Vanessa Lamorte Hartshorn

HOW TO USE

Below are some ideas for how to work with this journal :

Journaling is good for anchoring your overall experience. You may wish to use this journal for dreams, intention-setting, prayers, wishes, conscious programming, etc. It doesn't have to be one thing or another... how do you see yourself working with this tool?

Each week there is an image with keywords and reflections. The images are imbued with energy medicine that will be just right for y o u. To receive, use your own sensory guidance system (touch, smell, gaze, hearing, taste, etc.). Beyond that, sense into your part within the collective.

We intended to have inner child work woven throughout the year. A benefit of going into the inner child might be to make peace both internally and externally. When you engage with any tool, it is likely important to notice how your own creativity wants to come through. If you sense any type of authority, it may be of use to first feel into that word, 'authority.' Notice your response... process and feel into safety.

In connection with that inner child weaving, we decided to focus on planetary retrogrades this year. Retrogrades are all about reevaluation, reexamination - think 're-' words! In revisiting earlier times in our lives (eg, childhood, a certain year, etc.), we open ourselves up to potentially r e w r i t i n g any type of story attached to the initial experience. What would you rehash? Remember to have fun, to play, to create!

THE PLATONIC SOLIDS

Every image you see in this journal comes out of a circle or sphere : the Void (Child). Below is a list of the other 5 Platonic solids + what these building blocks to the Universe may suggest for you...

Fire (Male) - Tetrahedron

Left side of the brain, simplification, getting back to basics, natural Light, roles and cycles

Earth (Male) - Hexahedron

Left side of the brain, dynamic energy, expansion, connecting dots, finding patterns

Air (Child) - Octahedron

First form out of the Void, corpus callosum, links the left + right brain, main components for overall Creation, Time + Space

Water (Female) - Icosahedron

Right side of the brain, meteorites, anti-gravity elements, propulsion, thrust, cellular movement, change as a constant

Ether (Female) - Dodecahedron

Highest form of consciousness, DNA, blueprinting for life

RETROGRADES

We've included a list of the main retrograde cycles for all of 2021 here, as well as each week along the way. You may be wondering why some planets or asteroids or other astrological elements are not included. First off, some things do not appear as retrograde motion (eg, the Sun, the Moon). Second, some planetary bodies that are closer to the Sun have certain cycles, which do not show up each calendar year. For example, while Venus goes retrograde this year, Mars does not. Both have a roughly-every-two-years-or-so retrograde cycle; the next time they will be retrograde in the same calendar year will be in 2022!

:: 2021 Retrograde Calendar (Pacific Time) ::

Mercury

January 30th to February 20th, 2021

May 29th to June 22nd, 2021

September 26th to October 18th, 2021

Venus

December 19th, 2021 to January 29th, 2022

Jupiter

June 20th to October 17th, 2021

Saturn

May 23rd to October 10th, 2021

Uranus

August 15th, 2020 to January 14th, 2021

August 19th, 2021 to January 18th, 2022

Neptune

June 25th to December 1st, 2021

Pluto

April 27th to October 6th, 2021

 Polaris

January 1st - January 2nd

Retrograde :: Uranus

Keywords - True North, guidance

Where do you see yourself heading this year? How can you revisit what safety feels like?

_____
_____
_____
_____
_____
_____
_____
_____
_____
_____
_____
_____
_____
_____
_____
_____
_____
_____
_____
_____
_____
_____
_____
_____
_____

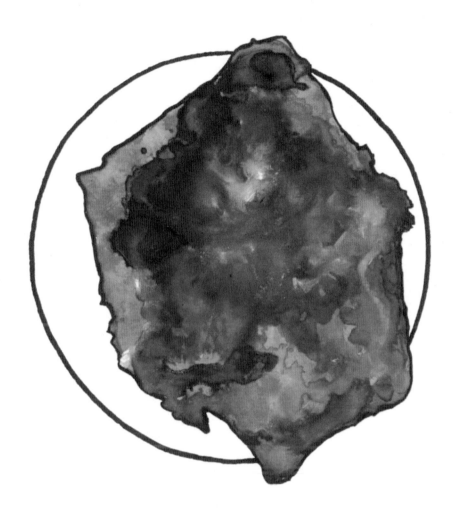

 Emerald

January 3rd - January 9th

Retrograde :: Uranus

Keywords - heart abundance, richness

How can you sink into your heart? What might it feel like for it to bloom?

_____

_____

_____

_____

_____

_____

_____

_____

_____

_____

_____

_____

_____

_____

_____

_____

_____

_____

_____

_____

_____

_____

_____

_____

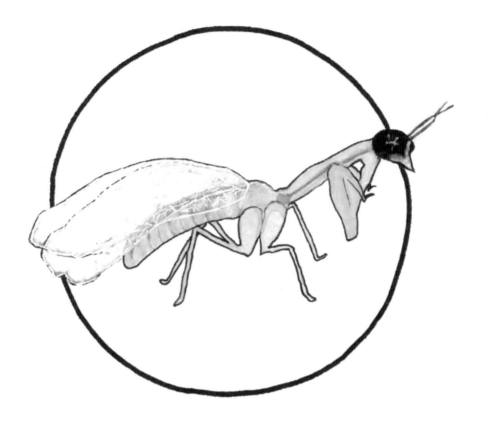

 Mantisfly

January 10th - January 16th

Retrograde :: Uranus direct 1/14

Keywords - revival, evolution, digging

Where might you be called to excavate something in
your life? How would it feel to go there?

_____
_____
_____
_____
_____
_____
_____
_____
_____
_____
_____
_____
_____
_____
_____
_____
_____
_____
_____
_____
_____
_____
_____
_____
_____
_____

 Skunk

January 17th - January 23rd

Keywords - boundaries, integration

Where is the biggest polarity in your life? What would it feel like to find the grey? Sniff it out.

_____

_____

_____

_____

_____

_____

_____

_____

_____

_____

_____

_____

_____

_____

_____

_____

_____

_____

_____

_____

_____

_____

_____

_____

_____

_____

_____

 Wolf

January 24th - January 30th

Retrograde :: Mercury begins 1/30

Keywords - inner howl, solitude

What part of your voice has been quieted? Where
have you been silent, and where do you need to
speak? Give yourself permission.

_____

_____

_____

_____

_____

_____

_____

_____

_____

_____

_____

_____

_____

_____

_____

_____

_____

_____

_____

_____

_____

_____

_____

 Amanita Muscaria

January 31st - February 6th

Retrograde :: Mercury

Keywords - crepuscular, eccentric, dance

How can you embrace spontaneity? Does your dream
life include laughter?

_____

_____

_____

_____

_____

_____

_____

_____

_____

_____

_____

_____

_____

_____

_____

_____

_____

_____

_____

_____

_____

_____

_____

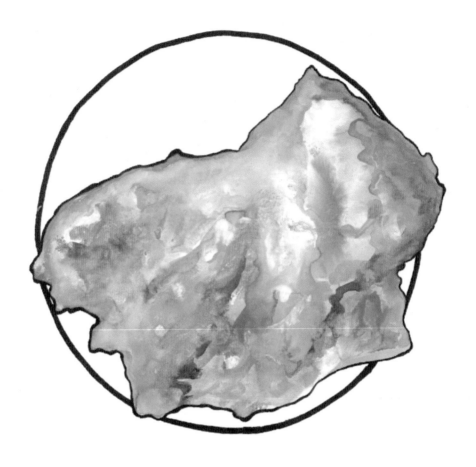

 Turquoise

February 7th - February 13th

Retrograde :: Mercury

Keywords - Divine Self, travel, astrals

Where would you go to find wholeness? What pieces would you leave behind + what pieces would you retrieve?

_____
_____
_____
_____
_____
_____
_____
_____
_____
_____
_____
_____
_____
_____
_____
_____
_____
_____
_____
_____
_____
_____
_____

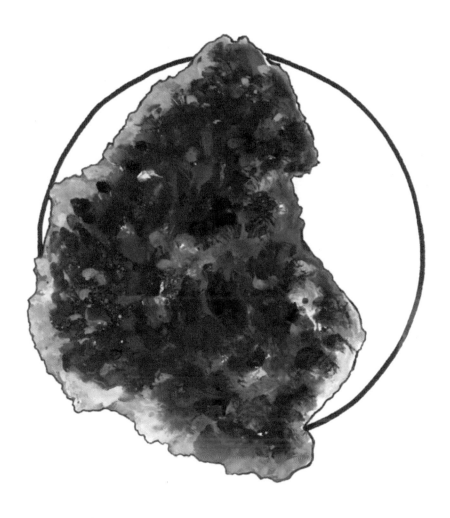

 Amethyst

February 14th - February 20th

Retrograde :: Mercury direct 2/20

Keywords - inspirational, channel, contact

Imagine being on a river... what one word would you use to describe the experience? What current of consciousness are you flowing with?

_____

_____

_____

_____

_____

_____

_____

_____

_____

_____

_____

_____

_____

_____

_____

_____

_____

_____

_____

_____

_____

_____

_____

_____

_____

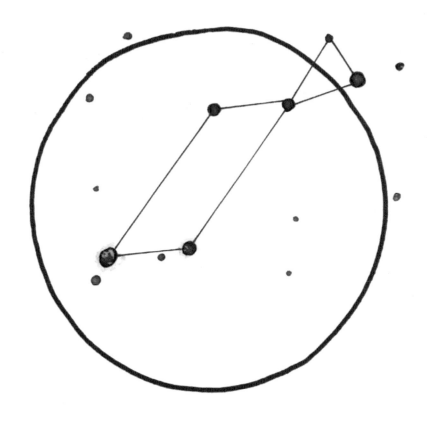

 Lyra

February 21st - February 27th

Keywords - harp, harmonic, hippocampus

What song would be playing in the background of your victory dance?

_____

_____

_____

_____

_____

_____

_____

_____

_____

_____

_____

_____

_____

_____

_____

_____

_____

_____

_____

_____

_____

_____

_____

_____

_____

 Zebra

February 28th - March 6th

Keywords - stand out, show your stripes

What makes you come alive? Would a group
strengthen your resolve?

_____
_____
_____
_____
_____
_____
_____
_____
_____
_____
_____
_____
_____
_____
_____
_____
_____
_____
_____
_____
_____
_____
_____
_____
_____
_____
_____
_____
_____
_____

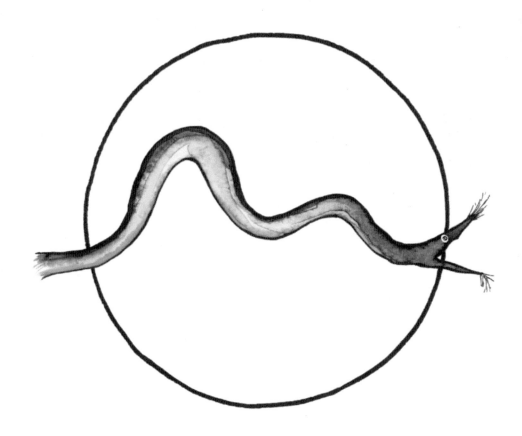

 Ribbon Eel

March 7th - March 13th

Keywords - non-binary, honing

If you were to name this phase of your life, what might you call it? What next chapter is writing you?

_____

_____

_____

_____

_____

_____

_____

_____

_____

_____

_____

_____

_____

_____

_____

_____

_____

_____

_____

_____

_____

_____

_____

_____

_____

_____

_____

_____

_____

_____

_____

 Millipede

March 14th - March 20th

Keywords - psychic sensitivity, temperature

What next move are you gauging?

_____

_____

_____

_____

_____

_____

_____

_____

_____

_____

_____

_____

_____

_____

_____

_____

_____

_____

_____

_____

_____

_____

_____

_____

_____

_____

_____

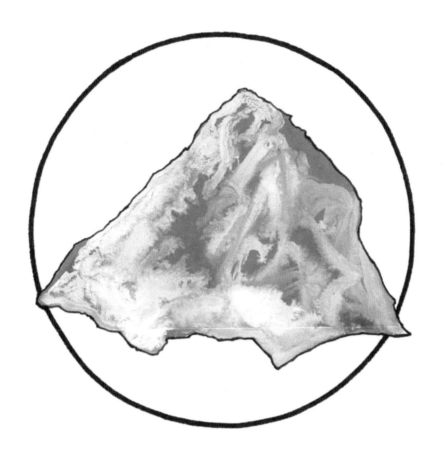

 Silver

March 21st - March 27th

Keywords - yin, far-reaching, threaded

What quiet strength do you possess? Do you realize
how interwoven your life is with the life around you?

_____

_____

_____

_____

_____

_____

_____

_____

_____

_____

_____

_____

_____

_____

_____

_____

_____

_____

_____

_____

_____

_____

_____

_____

_____

_____

_____

 Mosquito

March 28th - April 3rd

Keywords - vampiric, undetectable, detox

Who or what is sucking your energy? Have you even noticed? Reclaim sobriety.

_____

_____

_____

_____

_____

_____

_____

_____

_____

_____

_____

_____

_____

_____

_____

_____

_____

_____

_____

_____

_____

_____

_____

_____

_____

_____

_____

 Butterfly

April 4th - April 10th

How are you being conscious with social media? How is it transforming you + how are you transforming it?

_____

_____

_____

_____

_____

_____

_____

_____

_____

_____

_____

_____

_____

_____

_____

_____

_____

_____

_____

_____

_____

_____

_____

_____

_____

_____

_____

_____

_____

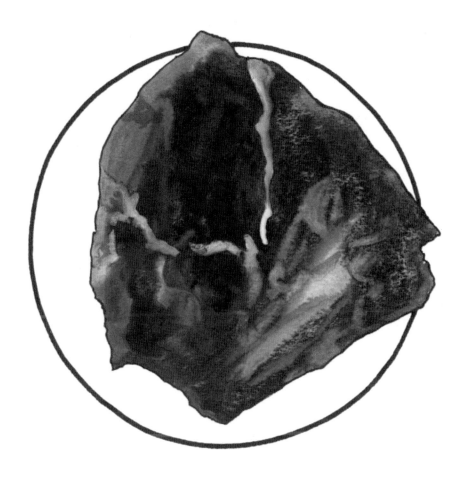

 Shungite

April 11th - April 17th

Keywords - electromagnetic, shielding

What in your life feels harmful? What practice is calling to you to reduce harm? How do you want to absorb?

_____

_____

_____

_____

_____

_____

_____

_____

_____

_____

_____

_____

_____

_____

_____

_____

_____

_____

_____

_____

_____

_____

_____

 Bee

April 18th - April 24th

Keywords - keeper, care, inner circle

Who are your people? How can you cultivate more symbiotic relationships?

_____

_____

_____

_____

_____

_____

_____

_____

_____

_____

_____

_____

_____

_____

_____

_____

_____

_____

_____

_____

_____

_____

_____

_____

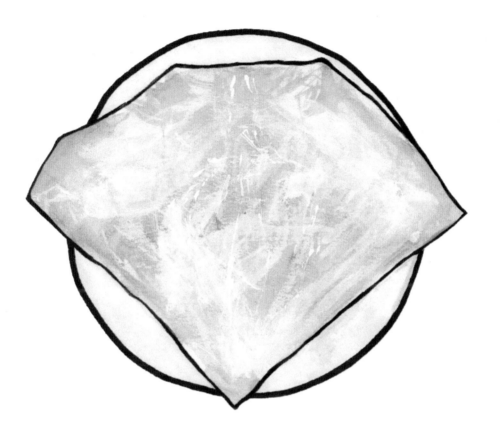

 Diamond

April 25th - May 1st

Retrograde :: Pluto begins 4/27

Keywords - refinement, polishing, Buddhic

Notice where you engage with playing the role of
savior. How do you work with pressure?

_____

_____

_____

_____

_____

_____

_____

_____

_____

_____

_____

_____

_____

_____

_____

_____

_____

_____

_____

_____

_____

_____

_____

_____

_____

_____

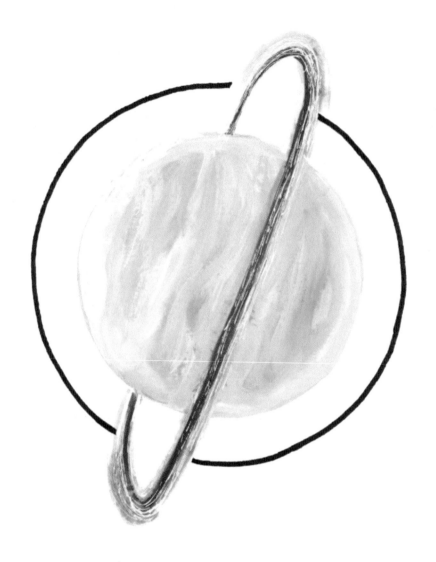

 Uranus

May 2nd - May 8th

Retrograde :: Pluto

Keywords - innovation, revolution, progression

How can you break the chains? How can you lean into your genius + creativity?

_____

_____

_____

_____

_____

_____

_____

_____

_____

_____

_____

_____

_____

_____

_____

_____

_____

_____

_____

_____

_____

_____

_____

_____

 Magnolia

May 9th - May 15th

Retrograde :: Pluto

Keywords - free will, perseverance

What would it feel like to breathe as if you never
breathed before? It's OK to take up space.

_____

_____

_____

_____

_____

_____

_____

_____

_____

_____

_____

_____

_____

_____

_____

_____

_____

_____

_____

_____

_____

_____

_____

_____

_____

_____

 Elephant

May 16th - May 22nd

Retrograde :: Pluto

Keywords - naiveté, trust, compassion

You didn't know then what you know now. Could
forgiveness serve you?

_____
_____
_____
_____
_____
_____
_____
_____
_____
_____
_____
_____
_____
_____
_____
_____
_____
_____
_____
_____
_____
_____
_____
_____
_____
_____
_____

 Thunderbird

May 23rd - May 29th

Retrograde :: Pluto, Saturn begins 5/23 &

Mercury begins 5/29

Keywords - myth, reality, tradition, fantasy

What legend are you claiming? Where are you needing acknowledgment? Recognize the Love in you, and see the Love in Others.

_____

_____

_____

_____

_____

_____

_____

_____

_____

_____

_____

_____

_____

_____

_____

_____

_____

_____

_____

_____

_____

_____

_____

_____

_____

_____

_____

 Cicada

May 30th - June 5th

Retrograde :: Pluto, Saturn, Mercury

Keywords - cycles, patience, brewing

Where is your sanctuary? What are you crafting there? Stir the pot.

_____

_____

_____

_____

_____

_____

_____

_____

_____

_____

_____

_____

_____

_____

_____

_____

_____

_____

_____

_____

_____

_____

_____

_____

 Sea Turtle

June 6th - June 12th

Retrograde :: Pluto, Saturn, Mercury

Keywords - transmutation, mutant, dragon, faith

What are you carrying on your back? Does it feel heavy? Light? Something else?

_____
_____
_____
_____
_____
_____
_____
_____
_____
_____
_____
_____
_____
_____
_____
_____
_____
_____
_____
_____
_____
_____
_____
_____
_____
_____
_____

 Ladybug

June 13th - June 19th

Retrograde :: Pluto, Saturn, Mercury

Keywords - wish, luck, multiply

What was your dream as a child? In the now, can you
wish upon a star?

_____

_____

_____

_____

_____

_____

_____

_____

_____

_____

_____

_____

_____

_____

_____

_____

_____

_____

_____

_____

_____

_____

_____

_____

_____

 Hot Poker Lily

June 20th - June 26th

Retrograde :: Pluto, Saturn, Mercury direct 6/22 &
Jupiter begins 6/20 & Neptune begins 6/25

Keywords - grandfather, bittersweet, absence

What are you grieving? Where are you detached? It
may feel relentless, but anger is a part of life.

_____
_____
_____
_____
_____
_____
_____
_____
_____
_____
_____
_____
_____
_____
_____
_____
_____
_____
_____
_____
_____
_____
_____

 Fairy

June 27th - July 3rd

Retrograde :: Pluto, Saturn, Jupiter, Neptune

Keywords - alien, embodiment, authenticity

Where in your life do you feel like you don't belong?
What would it feel like to be fully confident?

_____

_____

_____

_____

_____

_____

_____

_____

_____

_____

_____

_____

_____

_____

_____

_____

_____

_____

_____

_____

_____

_____

_____

_____

_____

 Grass

July 4th - July 10th

Retrograde :: Pluto, Saturn, Jupiter, Neptune

Keywords - simplicity, unconsciousness

What are you taking for granted in your life? What is in the foreground + what is in the background? Focus.

_____

_____

_____

_____

_____

_____

_____

_____

_____

_____

_____

_____

_____

_____

_____

_____

_____

_____

_____

_____

_____

_____

_____

_____

_____

_____

 Coral

July 11th - July 17th

Retrograde :: Pluto, Saturn, Jupiter, Neptune

Keywords - regeneration, colony

What needs revitalizing? How can you reignite the
basics of your vibrancy?

_____
_____
_____
_____
_____
_____
_____
_____
_____
_____
_____
_____
_____
_____
_____
_____
_____
_____
_____
_____
_____
_____
_____
_____
_____

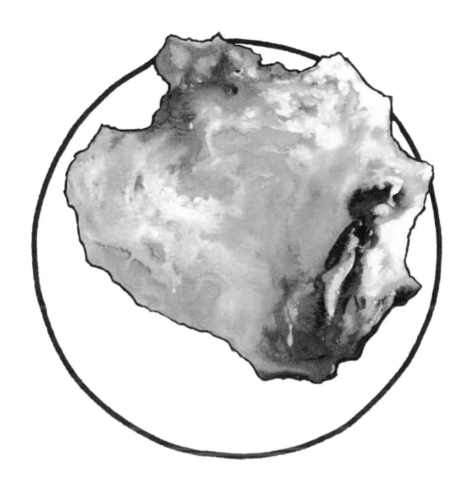

 Carnelian

July 18th - July 24th

Retrograde :: Pluto, Saturn, Jupiter, Neptune

Keywords - inner child, creativity, Divine Will

How do you want to move with new Heart?

_____
_____
_____
_____
_____
_____
_____
_____
_____
_____
_____
_____
_____
_____
_____
_____
_____
_____
_____
_____
_____
_____
_____
_____
_____
_____
_____
_____
_____
_____

 Foxglove

July 25th - July 31st

Retrograde :: Pluto, Saturn, Jupiter, Neptune

Keywords - friendship, fertility, whimsy

What bell is ringing? Are you listening? What is your threshold?

_____
_____
_____
_____
_____
_____
_____
_____
_____
_____
_____
_____
_____
_____
_____
_____
_____
_____
_____
_____
_____
_____
_____
_____
_____
_____
_____

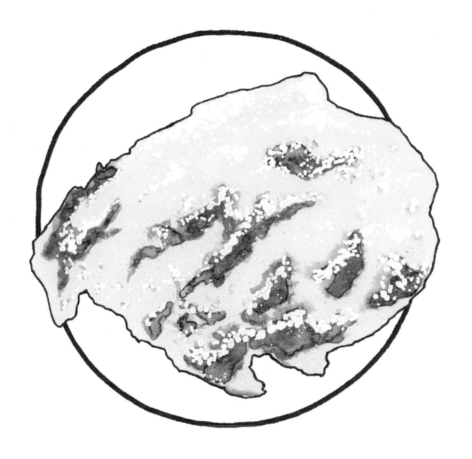

 Gold

August 1st - August 7th

Retrograde :: Pluto, Saturn, Jupiter, Neptune

Keywords - coronation, taking flight

How can you initiate yourself? What fuels your propulsion? You don't need to do gymnastics.

_____

_____

_____

_____

_____

_____

_____

_____

_____

_____

_____

_____

_____

_____

_____

_____

_____

_____

_____

_____

_____

_____

_____

_____

_____

_____

 Peacock

August 8th - August 14th

Retrograde :: Pluto, Saturn, Jupiter, Neptune

Keywords - regal, majestic, visionary

Show what you want to - whether someone is looking
or not. What does pride mean to you now?

_____

_____

_____

_____

_____

_____

_____

_____

_____

_____

_____

_____

_____

_____

_____

_____

_____

_____

_____

_____

_____

_____

_____

_____

Palm

August 15th - August 21st

Retrograde :: Pluto, Saturn, Jupiter, Neptune &

Uranus begins 8/19

Keywords - eternal, mutable, peace

How are you fanning yourself? Who is fanning you?
Stability comes through your own roots.

_____

_____

_____

_____

_____

_____

_____

_____

_____

_____

_____

_____

_____

_____

_____

_____

_____

_____

_____

_____

_____

_____

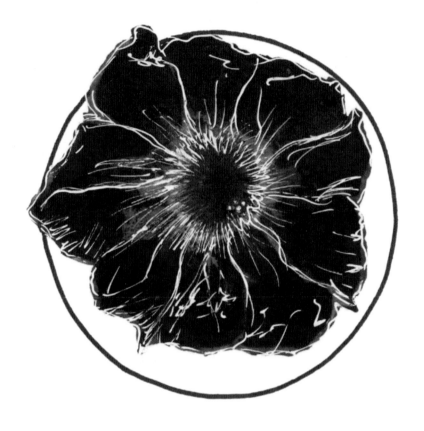

 Black Mamba Petunia

August 22nd - August 28th

Retrograde :: Pluto, Saturn, Jupiter, Neptune, Uranus

Keywords - cosmos, void, comfort

What question would Y O U ask this week?

_____

_____

_____

_____

_____

_____

_____

_____

_____

_____

_____

_____

_____

_____

_____

_____

_____

_____

_____

_____

_____

_____

_____

_____

_____

_____

_____

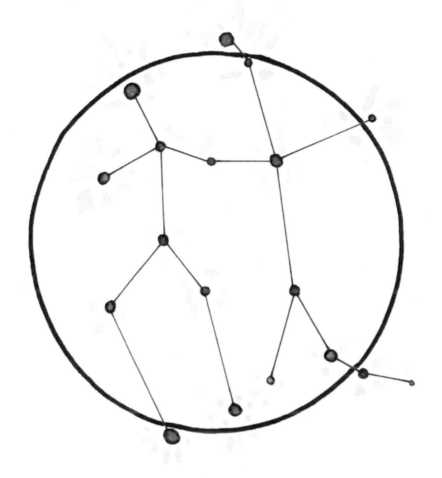

 Castor & Pollux

August 29th - September 4th

Retrograde :: Pluto, Saturn, Jupiter, Neptune, Uranus

Keywords - duality, projection, theatrical

What faces are you wearing? What faces do you
want to wear? How are you standing in your Self?

_____
_____
_____
_____
_____
_____
_____
_____
_____
_____
_____
_____
_____
_____
_____
_____
_____
_____
_____
_____
_____
_____
_____
_____
_____
_____
_____

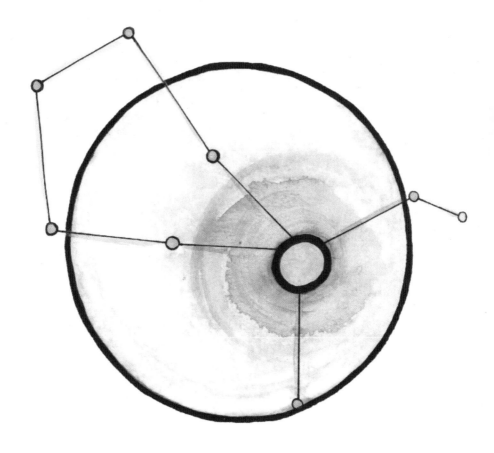

 Arcturus

September 5th - September 11th

Retrograde :: Pluto, Saturn, Jupiter, Neptune, Uranus

Keywords - equine, grace, purity

Where are you already fairly sensitive? Where would you like to become more sensitive?

_____

_____

_____

_____

_____

_____

_____

_____

_____

_____

_____

_____

_____

_____

_____

_____

_____

_____

_____

_____

_____

_____

_____

_____

_____

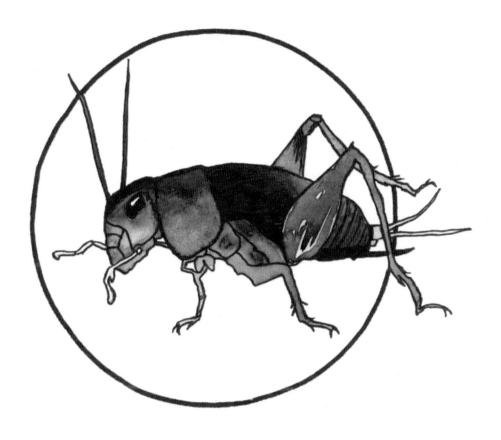

 Cricket

September 12th - September 18th

Retrograde :: Pluto, Saturn, Jupiter, Neptune, Uranus

Keywords - silence, mating, chorus

How can you be unapologetically you? Who or what
do you sing with most harmonically?

_____

_____

_____

_____

_____

_____

_____

_____

_____

_____

_____

_____

_____

_____

_____

_____

_____

_____

_____

_____

_____

_____

_____

_____

_____

_____

Bear

September 19th - September 25th

Retrograde :: Pluto, Saturn, Jupiter, Neptune, Uranus

Keywords - hunting, foresight, dexterity

Where do you feel closed off? How can you create access?

_____

_____

_____

_____

_____

_____

_____

_____

_____

_____

_____

_____

_____

_____

_____

_____

_____

_____

_____

_____

_____

_____

_____

_____

_____

_____

_____

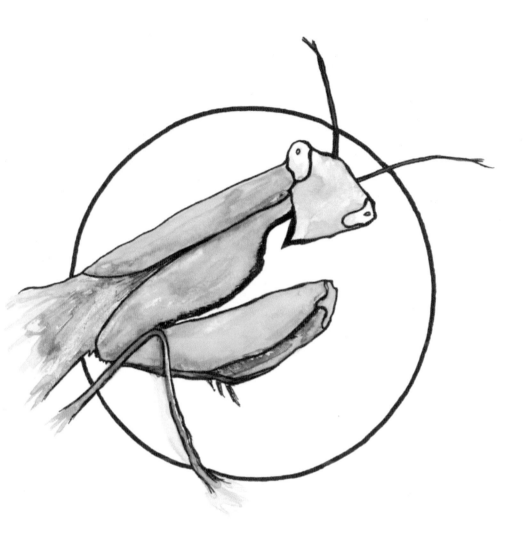

 Praying Mantis

September 26th - October 2nd

Retrograde :: Pluto, Saturn, Jupiter, Neptune, Uranus & Mercury begins 9/26

Keywords - stillness, zen, clarity

How can you engage with your innate ability to work with mind over matter?

_____

_____

_____

_____

_____

_____

_____

_____

_____

_____

_____

_____

_____

_____

_____

_____

_____

_____

_____

_____

_____

_____

_____

_____

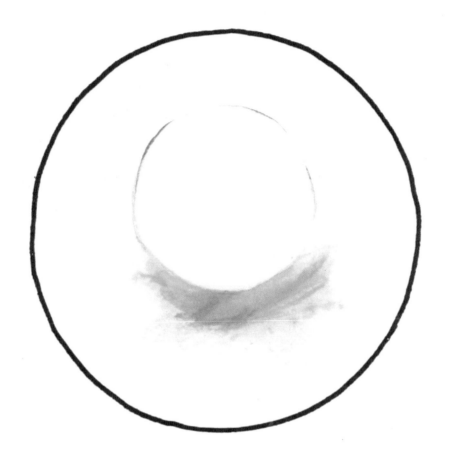

 Pearl

October 3rd - October 9th

Retrograde :: Saturn, Jupiter, Neptune, Uranus, Mercury & Pluto direct 10/6

Keywords - essence, distill, salty

Is there something reaching a breaking point in your life? What would it feel like to seed something new?

_____

_____

_____

_____

_____

_____

_____

_____

_____

_____

_____

_____

_____

_____

_____

_____

_____

_____

_____

_____

_____

_____

_____

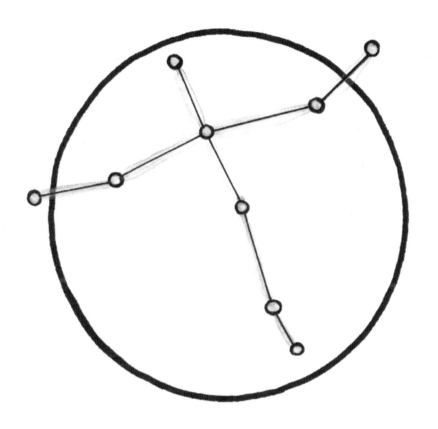

 Cygnus

October 10th - October 16th

Retrograde :: Jupiter, Neptune, Uranus, Mercury &
Saturn direct 10/10

Keywords - Switzerland, floating, veils

What have you been out-picturing recently? How does
the picture develop?

_____

_____

_____

_____

_____

_____

_____

_____

_____

_____

_____

_____

_____

_____

_____

_____

_____

_____

_____

_____

_____

_____

_____

 Kangaroo

October 17th - October 23rd

Retrograde :: Neptune, Uranus, Jupiter direct 10/17 &
Mercury direct 10/18

Keywords - underbelly, rocking, boxing, kicking

How can you come back into your body more? Do
you need to break out of a box?

_____

_____

_____

_____

_____

_____

_____

_____

_____

_____

_____

_____

_____

_____

_____

_____

_____

_____

_____

_____

_____

_____

_____

_____

 Milky Way

October 24th - October 30th

Retrograde :: Neptune, Uranus

Keywords - spiral, syzygy, density

What feels familiar? Have you been here before? Sink
or swim : how are you invited?

_____

_____

_____

_____

_____

_____

_____

_____

_____

_____

_____

_____

_____

_____

_____

_____

_____

_____

_____

_____

_____

_____

_____

_____

_____

_____

 Angel Oak

October 31st - November 6th

Retrograde :: Neptune, Uranus

Keywords - longevity, endurance, anchoring

Where have you been let down? How can you move from the personal to the transpersonal? There are angels around you.

_____

_____

_____

_____

_____

_____

_____

_____

_____

_____

_____

_____

_____

_____

_____

_____

_____

_____

_____

_____

_____

_____

_____

_____

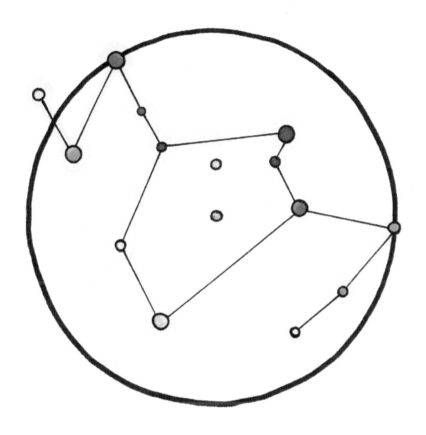

Phoenix

November 7th - November 13th

Retrograde :: Neptune, Uranus

Keywords - bless, rise, mercy

What would it feel like to remember your humanity?
If you were to answer your own prayers, what would
you do?

_____

_____

_____

_____

_____

_____

_____

_____

_____

_____

_____

_____

_____

_____

_____

_____

_____

_____

_____

_____

_____

_____

_____

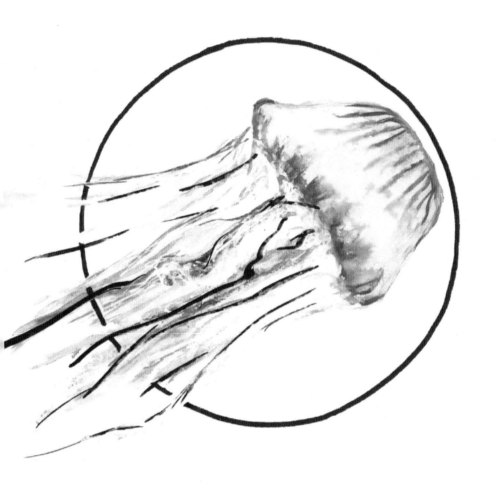

 Jellyfish

November 14th - November 20th

Retrograde :: Neptune, Uranus

Keywords - reactivity, mushrooms, exposed

Where do you feel naked? Where do you want to add, and where are you OK with subtraction?

_____
_____
_____
_____
_____
_____
_____
_____
_____
_____
_____
_____
_____
_____
_____
_____
_____
_____
_____
_____
_____
_____
_____
_____
_____
_____
_____

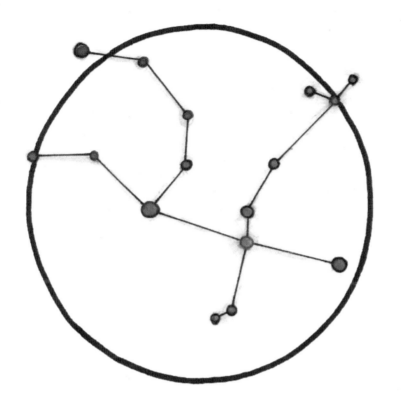

 Andromeda

November 21st - November 27th

Retrograde :: Neptune, Uranus

Keywords - compromise, negotiation, mediation

Notice the language you are choosing. Are you really sharing what's on your heart?

_____

_____

_____

_____

_____

_____

_____

_____

_____

_____

_____

_____

_____

_____

_____

_____

_____

_____

_____

_____

_____

_____

_____

_____

_____

_____

 Hummingbird

November 28th - December 4th

Retrograde :: Uranus, Neptune direct 12/1

Keywords - navigation, joy, peek-a-boo

Do you feel cradled? Do you also feel free? If not, how would you change what you see?

_____

_____

_____

_____

_____

_____

_____

_____

_____

_____

_____

_____

_____

_____

_____

_____

_____

_____

_____

_____

_____

_____

_____

_____

 Lapis Lazuli

December 5th - December 11th

Retrograde :: Uranus

Keywords - third eye, illumination, clairvoyance

What treasures are you finding? How are you panning
for gold?

_____

_____

_____

_____

_____

_____

_____

_____

_____

_____

_____

_____

_____

_____

_____

_____

_____

_____

_____

_____

_____

_____

_____

_____

_____

_____

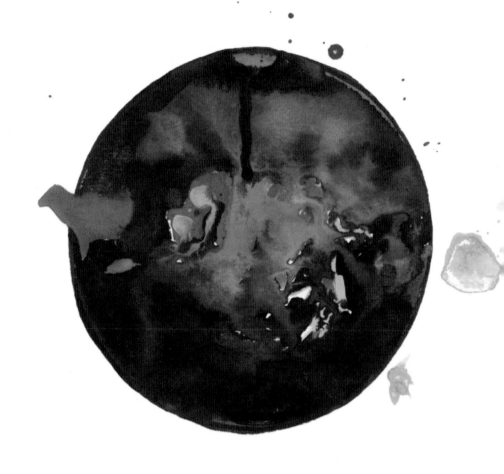

 Galactic Center

December 12th - December 18th

Retrograde :: Uranus

Keywords - conclusion, synthesis

What is coming to a close? Where are you needing
hibernation? Where are you holding out for rest?

_____

_____

_____

_____

_____

_____

_____

_____

_____

_____

_____

_____

_____

_____

_____

_____

_____

_____

_____

_____

_____

_____

_____

_____

_____

_____

 Pine

December 19th - December 25th

Retrograde :: Uranus, Venus begins 12/19

Keywords - pineal gland, telepathy, needles

How do you pinpoint resonance? Where are you camping out?

_____

_____

_____

_____

_____

_____

_____

_____

_____

_____

_____

_____

_____

_____

_____

_____

_____

_____

_____

_____

_____

_____

_____

_____

_____

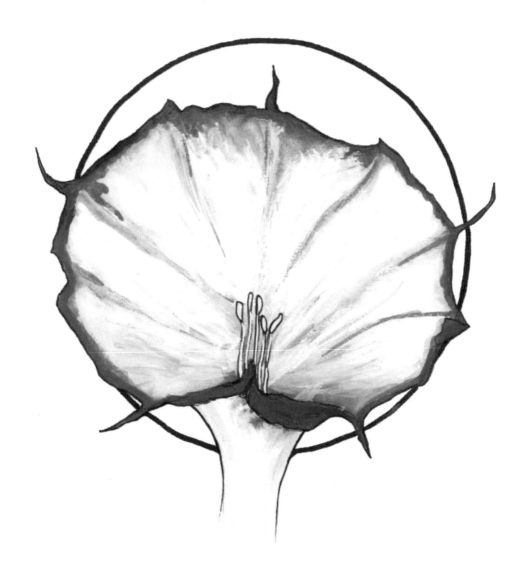

 Datura

December 26th - December 31st

Retrograde :: Uranus, Venus

Keywords - sage wisdom, trumpet, crone

What would you say to yourself now? What could
offer the most catharsis?

_____
_____
_____
_____
_____
_____
_____
_____
_____
_____
_____
_____
_____
_____
_____
_____
_____
_____
_____
_____
_____
_____
_____
_____
_____

Made in the USA
Middletown, DE
26 March 2021